Molly Pitcher

Heroine

Colonial Leaders

Lord Baltimore
English Politician and Colonist

Benjamin Banneker
American Mathematician and Astronomer

Sir William Berkeley
Governor of Virginia

William Bradford
Governor of Plymouth Colony

Jonathan Edwards
Colonial Religious Leader

Benjamin Franklin
American Statesman, Scientist, and Writer

Anne Hutchinson
Religious Leader

Cotton Mather
Author, Clergyman, and Scholar

Increase Mather
Clergyman and Scholar

James Oglethorpe
Humanitarian and Soldier

William Penn
Founder of Democracy

Sir Walter Raleigh
English Explorer and Author

Caesar Rodney
American Patriot

John Smith
English Explorer and Colonist

Miles Standish
Plymouth Colony Leader

Peter Stuyvesant
Dutch Military Leader

George Whitefield
Clergyman and Scholar

Roger Williams
Founder of Rhode Island

John Winthrop
Politician and Statesman

John Peter Zenger
Free Press Advocate

Revolutionary War Leaders

John Adams
Second U.S. President

Samuel Adams
Patriot

Ethan Allen
Revolutionary Hero

Benedict Arnold
Traitor to the Cause

John Burgoyne
British General

George Rogers Clark
American General

Lord Cornwallis
British General

Thomas Gage
British General

King George III
English Monarch

Nathanael Greene
Military Leader

Nathan Hale
Revolutionary Hero

Alexander Hamilton
First U.S. Secretary of the Treasury

John Hancock
President of the Continental Congress

Patrick Henry
American Statesman and Speaker

William Howe
British General

John Jay
First Chief Justice of the Supreme Court

Thomas Jefferson
Author of the Declaration of Independence

John Paul Jones
Father of the U.S. Navy

Thaddeus Kosciuszko
Polish General and Patriot

Lafayette
French Freedom Fighter

James Madison
Father of the Constitution

Francis Marion
The Swamp Fox

James Monroe
American Statesman

Thomas Paine
Political Writer

Molly Pitcher
Heroine

Paul Revere
American Patriot

Betsy Ross
American Patriot

Baron Von Steuben
American General

George Washington
First U.S. President

Anthony Wayne
American General

Famous Figures of the Civil War Era

John Brown
Abolitionist

Jefferson Davis
Confederate President

Frederick Douglass
Abolitionist and Author

Stephen A. Douglas
Champion of the Union

David Farragut
Union Admiral

Ulysses S. Grant
Military Leader and President

Stonewall Jackson
Confederate General

Joseph E. Johnston
Confederate General

Robert E. Lee
Confederate General

Abraham Lincoln
Civil War President

George Gordon Meade
Union General

George McClellan
Union General

William Henry Seward
Senator and Statesman

Philip Sheridan
Union General

William Sherman
Union General

Edwin Stanton
Secretary of War

Harriet Beecher Stowe
Author of Uncle Tom's Cabin

James Ewell Brown Stuart
Confederate General

Sojourner Truth
Abolitionist, Suffragist, and Preacher

Harriet Tubman
Leader of the Underground Railroad

Molly Pitcher

Heroine

Eileen Dunn Bertanzetti

Arthur M. Schlesinger, jr.
Senior Consulting Editor

Chelsea House Publishers

Philadelphia

CHELSEA HOUSE PUBLISHERS
Editor-in-Chief Sally Cheney
Director of Production Kim Shinners
Production Manager Pamela Loos
Art Director Sara Davis
Production Editor Diann Grasse

Staff for *MOLLY PITCHER*
Editor Sally Cheney
Associate Art Director Takeshi Takahashi
Series Design Keith Trego
Cover Design 21st Century Publishing and Communications, Inc.
Picture Researcher Pat Holl
Layout 21st Century Publishing and Communications, Inc.

The Chelsea House World Wide Web address is
http://www.chelseahouse.com

First Printing
1 3 5 7 9 8 6 4 2

Library of Congress Cataloging-in-Publication Data

Bertanzetti, Eileen Dunn.
    Molly Pitcher / Eileen Dunn Bertanzetti.
        p. cm. — (Revolutionary War leaders)
    Includes bibliographical references and index.
    ISBN 0-7910-6400-X (hc : alk. paper) — ISBN 0-7910-6401-8
    (pbk. : alk. paper)
        1. Pitcher, Molly, 1754-1832—Juvenile literature. 2. Monmouth,
    Battle of, 1778—Juvenile literature. 3. Women revolutionaries—
    United States—Biography—Juvenile literature. 4. Revolutionaries—
    United States—Biography—Juvenile literature. 5. United
    States—History—Revolution, 1775-1783—Biography—Juvenile
    literature. [1. Pitcher, Molly, 1754-1832. 2. Revolutionaries.
    3. Monmouth, Battle of, 1778. 4. United States—History—Revolu-
    tion, 1775-1783. 5. Women—Biography.] I. Title. II. Series.

E241.M7 B47 2001
973.3'34—dc21   2001028524

Publisher's Note: In Colonial and Revolutionary War America, there were no standard rules for spelling, punctuation, capitalization, or grammar. Some of the quotations that appear in the Colonial Leaders and Revolutionary War Leaders series come from original documents and letters written during this time in history. Original quotations reflect writing inconsistencies of the period.

Contents

Molly Ludwig was 22 years old when George Washington fought the Battle of Monmouth. The battle took place in an area not far from where Mary grew up.

Growing Up on a Farm

On her parents' farm in New Jersey around 1754, Mary Ludwig was born. Her parents had no idea she would one day earn herself a place in American history. They did not know people would one day call their daughter "Molly Pitcher."

Now, on her day of birth more than 30 years before New Jersey became a state, tiny Mary was lucky to be alive. Throughout the **colonies**, most children were born at home. No hospitals, doctors, or modern medicines helped poor farm families like the Ludwigs. In some places, almost half of all mothers and babies died during birth. Though her birth may have given her trouble, newborn Mary would find even greater dangers in the life that awaited her.

Most records say Mary's **ancestors** arrived in the colonies after a long journey that began in Germany. Much evidence supports Mary's German background. First, many colonists called the German **immigrants** the "Dutch." After Mary Ludwig died, her granddaughter Polly McCleester said Mary was as "Dutch as sauer krout." Also, Mary and many of her relatives attended the Lutheran Church in Carlisle, Pennsylvania. According to some records, the congregation was mostly German.

Mary's parents' early history was lost because of the troubles they experienced when they traveled to the colonies. Many colonists lost their early records when the British, French, and Indians burned their homes and villages. The British sometimes destroyed immigrants' records as a way to control those same people.

Also, the immigrants from different countries

spoke different languages. This confused colonial officials responsible for recording details about those individuals. Many immigrants could not read or write—or at least they could not do so in the "official" language used in the colonies. Therefore, many early records were never written down at all. Or if they *were* written down, the official may have written them the way they *sounded,* rather than the way they were actually spelled. For example, in some immigration records, Mary's last name "Ludwig" was also spelled "Ludewig" and "Ludwick."

Some historians even question Mary's year of birth. In Carlisle in 1876, citizens unveiled a monument that honored Mary. The monument reads:

"DIED JANUARY 22, 1833,
AGED SEVENTY-NINE YEARS"

That would mean she was born in 1754. Still, some say she died in 1832 at nearly 90 years old. That would mean she was born in 1742, twelve years earlier than the monument's date. But official records show Mary's birth happened between 1750 and 1755. And her official death notice comes close to the monument's date and age, so "around 1754" makes the most sense.

Historians do agree Mary Ludwig was a real person. And they know that her parents, like the hundreds of thousands of other immigrants, hoped to find a better life in the colonies. They wanted a new life in which they would not suffer pain, hardship, and poverty.

But many immigrants did not even survive their first year in the colonies. Among other tragedies, they suffered the horrors of colonial warfare. Britain and France fought to own and rule the colonies. These countries often used American Indians to torture and kill the colonists.

Somehow, Mary's parents avoided bloodshed as they settled their plot of gently rolling land near Trenton in the New Jersey colony. They had chosen to live near the mighty Delaware River. It separated New Jersey from

This British cartoon criticizes Britain's use of American Indians in the British war with France to own and rule the colonies.

the Pennsylvania colony. The river and its streams provided plenty of water for the Ludwigs' farm animals and crops. The river also acted as a highway. It allowed the transporting of goods to and from Trenton, today the capital of New Jersey.

Mary could not have known that by the time she was 22 years old the place where she lived would no longer be peaceful. General George Washington would cross the Delaware and win the Battle of Trenton, near her parents' farm. By the time Mary was almost 24, she would be struggling in the smoke and storm of gunfire. She would hear the cries of war at the Battle of Monmouth, not far from Trenton.

But it was best that Mary did not know the future. The present time brought enough troubles. Mary's parents were busy struggling to keep their cows and crops healthy enough to produce food for their own use and to sell to other colonists. In the process, the Ludwigs built up their own strength of body and mind. This helped them survive the diseases that tore through the colonies, killing thousands of immigrants and Native Americans.

Mrs. Ludwig's knowledge of homemade remedies helped her to treat many of her family's illnesses. During Mary's childhood, she learned from her mother how to use these medicines to help people.

Throughout Mary's childhood, most poor farm girls like herself never received formal schooling. For one thing, their families could not afford it. Like Mary, those farm girls spent their childhood learning to cook, clean, grow vegetables, and tend the family's livestock. The girls learned to make soap, fabric, clothes, and candles. Though some records claim Mary could not write, most girls learned from their mothers how to read at least well enough to study the Bible.

Mary had no spare time to attend school, even if her parents could have afforded to send her. They needed her help to keep their farm going so they would not lose it and starve, as many immigrants had.

During Mary's growing-up years, homemakers like Mrs. Ludwig had to work from sunup to sundown. All the food for a farm family was homemade and cooked over a fireplace. On the busy colonial farm, there were eggs to gather, butter to churn, and bread to

To show their support of the Revolutionary War, colonists were expected to make their own yarn, fabric, and clothing. Some people used wool to make these goods. After the people shaved the wool off their sheep, children had to spend hours picking chunks of dried dirt out of the wool. Women and older children would spin the clean wool into yarn. But before they used the yarn to make fabric for the family's clothing, they might dye—color—the yarn. They made dyes from nuts, flowers, berries, vegetables, and roots. They even used soot from the fireplace to create dye.

bake. Farm girls like Mary were expected to help their mothers in all of these tasks—and more.

By the time Mary reached her teen years, some records show that a doctor's wife from Carlisle, Pennsylvania, traveled by horse to Mary's area. One day the woman, Mrs. Anna Callender Irvine, happened to meet Mary. Anna watched sturdy Mary work at her daily chores.

The young girl's strength and skill must have impressed Mrs. Irvine. Mary was good at doing what colonists expected women and girls to do: "women's work." This included household chores, sewing, and cooking. Mrs. Irvine decided to ask Mary's parents if she could hire

A group of farm women and children return home after gathering grain from the fields.

their daughter. Anna Irvine wanted Mary to travel to Carlisle with her and work as the Irvines' servant.

The Ludwig's farm was 150 miles from Carlisle. The thought of losing her only child may have saddened Mrs. Ludwig. And with so much work to do every day, Mary's parents must have wanted to keep her with them. They needed Mary to continue to contribute to the running of the farm.

And how did Mary feel about leaving her childhood home? It would be difficult, at such a young age, to leave the two people who loved her most. Because her parents had always taught her how to work hard and to help others, Mary had grown strong in body, mind, and heart. She may have wanted to help the Irvines, but she must have also wanted to stay and help her parents. As one of her friends once said about Mary, "She was as kind-hearted" as anyone who ever lived.

On the other hand, if Mary moved to Carlisle to work for the Irvines, she would earn some money. She could then send it to her parents. Poor farmers like the Ludwigs always needed money. Mary also probably knew if she moved to Carlisle, her parents would have one less mouth to feed, one less responsibility.

Many colonial women like Mrs. Irvine hired strong girls like Mary to live and work in their homes. Extra hands could lighten a woman's workload, especially if those hands belonged to someone as well trained as Mary. It would take much courage for Mary to leave with Anna Irvine.

The peace treaty signed by Colonel Henry Bouquet and the Native Americans opened up trade between the settlers and the Indians.

Always a Servant

Mary and her parents had to decide what to do about Mrs. Irvine's proposal.

The Ludwigs may not have known how important Carlisle, Pennsylvania, was to the colonies. Long before Anna Irvine arrived at the Ludwig farm, Carlisle had been a center of military action. In Carlisle lay Fort Louther. During the French and Indian War, which ended when Mary was about 10 years old, Fort Louther protected women and children from Native Americans. These "savages," as some settlers called them, often attacked homesteads.

In Carlisle on July 13, 1763, Colonel Henry Bouquet

wrote to Pennsylvania's Governor James Hamilton about the "[acts] of the murders committed by the Savages in this unfortunate County." The Colonel continued, "The List of People known to be killed . . . increases very fast every Hour."

By 1764, Colonel Bouquet had made peace with the Indians, which ended the French and Indian War. The colonies forced the Indians to return the women and children they had captured. Officials often sent these captives to Carlisle where their families could find them and take them back home. Near Fort Louther, a trail led from Philadelphia to the western frontier. Even as late as 1794, troops met in Carlisle before starting their march along this trail. In fact, in 1794, George Washington journeyed to Carlisle to encourage the troops.

The possibility of going to Carlisle with Anna Irvine probably excited Mary. The town may have seemed a more likely place in which to find adventure than did the Ludwigs' farm. But if Mary could have known the troubles that

The kitchen was a busy place in colonial times. There were many tasks to be done while preparing meals for the family. Mary would be a helpful addition to the Irvine household.

awaited her in Carlisle, she may have decided to stay with her parents.

Mary probably had not known that the hard farm life of her childhood had prepared her for an even more difficult life ahead. But almost as soon as she met Mary, Anna Irvine must have known that this sturdy girl with the honest face would serve her well back in Carlisle. Anna knew Mary would do a fine job at whatever task given her, whether it was scrubbing a floor, washing dishes and clothes, or cooking. A friend of hers once said about Mary, "She was of average height, muscular, strong. . . ."

And Mrs. Irvine probably believed she could trust Mary because many immigrants came from strict religious backgrounds. Some records say Mary was a Christian of the Lutheran faith.

Mary's parents decided to allow her to move to Carlisle. According to some records, Anna Irvine probably used horses to carry herself and the girl along the rough trail to Mary's new home. Today, by car or bus, it would take only about three hours to reach Carlisle from the Ludwigs' New Jersey farm. But in Mary's day, colonists could travel only by horse, ox, wagon, stagecoach, boat, or on foot. With Mrs. Irvine's horses, it might have taken Mary and her more than a week of hard and dangerous traveling to reach Carlisle.

The trail between Trenton and Carlisle snaked up and down many hills and mountains. Part of the trail may have followed old Indian paths. The trail wound around swamps. Mary and Anna had to cross three major rivers and many smaller ones. They probably depended on other people to ferry them across the deeper, wider, faster-moving waters.

Even though the French and Indian War had ended with a peace treaty before Mary left New Jersey, many dangers still lurked on the long journey to Carlisle. The sight of a bear or lightning could cause the horses to race in the wrong direction. If the horses injured themselves, Anna and Mary would have to walk, leading the horses the rest of the way. And even if the horses remained strong and healthy during the entire trip, the animals needed frequent rest periods. A flood could delay Anna and Mary's crossing of one of the rivers. And there was always the chance of getting lost along the trail. All of this could slow their journey—or end it.

Mary and Anna traveled by horse to Carlisle. The animals had to be properly cared for to ensure safe passage for the women.

But records show Anna and Mary *did* make it to Carlisle. In fact, according to many historians, Mary spent the last 40 years of her life in that busy town.

When Mary first arrived in Carlisle, a quarry lay just outside the town. From this deep, wide hole, men dug stone to use in building the Carlisle prison. In the prison, the colonial military would house British soldiers taken prisoner during war. In one building near Carlisle, people manufactured **muskets**, **ramrods**, and other weapons for war.

During the French and Indian War, Carlisle households had manufactured–by hand–cloth, clothing, and shoes for themselves and the army. At that time, the British king, George III, had promised free land to anyone who would build **flourmills** to grind grain for the army. Mary may have noticed the many mills still operating along the creeks of Carlisle. This town, with all its activity and strong **Patriots**, promised excitement.

By the time Mary arrived in Carlisle, its colonists and Indians no longer tried to kill each other as they had done for years. They could now be seen helping each other in their everyday work. In 1764, a few years before Mary arrived, Colonel Henry Bouquet had made this possible by signing a peace treaty with the Indians.

The presence of Carlisle's fort, distinguished military leaders, and well-trained soldiers must have given Mary a sense of security in her new home. And the presence of Carlisle's many religious people would have assured her that the values she had learned would be encouraged here.

Almost as soon as Mary arrived at Dr. William Irvine's home, Mrs. Irvine probably put her to work. If Mary had hoped to do more exciting chores here than she had done on her parents' farm, she would have been disappointed. She did only the most humble tasks in her new home. She scrubbed steps, scoured pots, and washed—by hand—the family's clothes. According to Caroline Ege, who lived in Carlisle all her life, Mary Ludwig "was hired to do the most **menial** work..."

When Dr. Irvine was not treating his patients,

he spent a lot of time on military matters. During the Revolutionary War, he earned the rank of colonel and then brigadier general.

Many in Carlisle, including the doctor, were angry because the British king had decided to tax goods like glass, paper, and tea, which the colonists needed. In 1773, Dr. Irvine heard how colonists in Boston had protested these taxes by throwing boxes of tea from ships into Boston Harbor. This "Boston Tea Party" caused the British to close the harbor. The colonists were sending a message to King George III that the taxes and laws he imposed would no longer be tolerated.

During the Revolutionary War, Margaret Corbin, a young woman about Molly's age, followed the troops. When Margaret was still a child, Native Americans killed her father and captured her mother. After that, Margaret's uncle raised her. During the war, gunfire killed Margaret's husband John while he worked his cannon. Margaret took his place and began to fire at enemy soldiers. During the battle, enemy bullets ripped open her arm and chest, but she lived for many years after that. After Margaret died, people who wanted to honor her bravery buried her at the United States Military Academy at West Point.

The colonial attitudes toward women and their role in society was about to change with the start of the Revolutionary War.

3

Peace Turns to War

On July 12, 1774, in the Presbyterian Church in Carlisle, Dr. William Irvine and other men met to decide what to do to help their "suffering **brethren** in Boston." During this meeting, Irvine and the others decided to show their support for Boston. They decided to order the Carlisle citizens not to buy or use any goods from Britain and not to sell any colonial goods to the British.

That evening, Dr. Irvine and the others created a list of men that would make sure the citizens carried out the orders. William Irvine appeared on that list.

Colonial society had most often thought women

should not participate in political matters. That attitude would soon begin to change. Women, including young Mary Ludwig, would need to take a stand on whether or not to support the "suffering brethren in Boston" and elsewhere in the colonies.

But a few years before the Boston Tea Party, in 1769, Mary did not need to make that decision. She was still doing "women's work," laboring hard for the Irvine family. According to one report, while Mary was "sweeping in front of the [Irvine] home," she managed to catch the attention of a young Carlisle barber as he passed her. Though many historians say Mary Ludwig "was not very attractive," most agree she was kindhearted and helpful to the sick and needy.

Mary's eagerness to do good for others might have been what won the young barber's heart. William Hays, born in Ireland, soon asked her to marry him. On July 24, 1769, they married in the Irvines' large home. Many years later on that same location, Carlisle built the First Lutheran

Church, to which Mary belonged.

Now people called Mary Ludwig "Mrs. Mary Hays." In the 1700s, married women had control over their household work, but society expected them to keep quiet in other matters. All the years on her parents' farm and in Dr. Irvine's home had trained Mary to perform the duties expected of a homemaker.

The next year, 1770, the British killed five colonists in the Boston Massacre. This made the colonists angrier than ever about being ruled by Britain. Also, Americans were still angry about paying taxes to England for tea and other goods. They wanted to know why they should give tax money to a king who lived thousands of miles away, across the Atlantic Ocean. It was during Mary's fourth year of marriage, in 1773, that the Boston Tea Party occurred.

The colonists had no modern means of communication with which they could quickly get information to each other. But they did have riders on horseback throughout the 13 colonies.

On March 5, 1770, British soldiers and colonists
fought in what would be called the Boston Massacre.
Five colonists were killed in the confrontation.

These messengers delivered news about Britain's
activities. Because of these riders, in April 1775,
citizens of Carlisle, including Mary and William
Hays, knew that a new war had started. In that

month, the Battles of Lexington and Concord in Massachusetts started the Revolutionary War. As always, many citizens of Carlisle were ready to join the fight for America's freedom.

The French and Indian War had made many well-trained soldiers out of Carlisle's citizens. Distinguished military leaders, like Colonel William Irvine, lived there. Households could still manufacture clothing for the army, and the mills could still grind grain for the soldiers. The town could still manufacture weapons and ammunition, too.

In June 1775, the Continental Congress appointed George Washington as commander in chief of the Continental Army. Also during June, Congress responded to the need for more soldiers to fight the new war. The Congress voted to raise 10 companies of expert riflemen. Two of those companies would come from Carlisle.

When Mary's young husband prepared to fight as part of the Continental Army, she must have seen the fire of patriotism in his eyes. For many reasons, that same patriotism must have been growing inside her too.

In Mary's parents' colony in New Jersey, British soldiers had recently forced their way into many homes. These men had physically abused the women there. Sometimes the soldiers had even killed them and their husbands. Often the British would steal the colonists' crops and kill their farm animals. The soldiers would then use these goods as food for the British troops. News of this caused Mary to worry about the safety of her parents.

At this time in Carlisle, many citizens obeyed the orders of Colonel Irvine and the others. These orders commanded the people not to buy or use any goods from Britain and not to sell any colonial goods to the British. In this way, colonists could show their anger over the unfair taxation.

Because of these orders, many women, in addition to their heavy load of daily chores, gathered together in "spinning bees." They spun thread on their spinning wheels. With this thread they wove a fabric called "homespun." To show support of all the colonists who opposed the crown, they made their families' clothing from this coarse fabric. Then they did not have to purchase British-made fabric and clothing. But those who wore the homespun also had to make sacrifices. Unlike the fine, smooth British-made fabrics, homespun's rough surfaces scratched the skin. It also did not look as good as Britain's finer fabrics. But many colonists chose to make this sacrifice in order to help gain freedom from the British.

Although colonial women were not expected to take part in political matters, the spinning bees produced more than homespun. They gave the women, like Mary Hays, the opportunity to discuss what was happening between Britain and the colonies. The heated discussions between the women at these "bees" also stirred up their desire to help in the war effort.

In addition to these influences on Mary, some colonial women had already broken out of the "mold" society had forced on them. Women who lived close to the battlefronts often acted as spies and carried messages across enemy lines. Women sometimes hid soldiers in their homes so the enemy would not find them.

In Carlisle and elsewhere in the colonies, **recruiters** came to town to try to get men to join the Continental Army. With their parents' permission, even 14 year old boys could join. To gain the attention of as many people as possible, the recruiters would stand in the middle of town and wave colorful banners in the air. They had musicians playing patriotic marches. The recruiters would tell the men and boys why they should join the army. The recruiters would even fire muskets or cannons to gain attention. And their speeches would include many spiteful remarks about King George III.

Though colonial society did not believe women should fight in wars, the recruiters' performances attracted a few women. These women would disguise themselves as men, join the army, and serve as men during the Revolutionary War.

Colonial women also showed their support of the troops in other ways. Some women helped make musket balls out of their metal dishes and statues. Some women carried supplies to the troops, while others brought food and comfort to colonial soldiers jailed by the British.

These patriotic activities of colonial women influenced others. These activities made women, like Mary Hays, want to do all they could to help in America's struggle for **independence**.

When William Hays left Carlisle to fight in George Washington's Continental Army, he served under the command of Mary's boss,

In 1775, 15 year old John Greenwood decided to play the fife—a small flute—in the Continental Army. During the war, his music encouraged the soldiers. When his military service ended, John headed home. Sickness had left him so weak he could barely hobble along the rough trail. Hundreds of insect bites had left his skin raw. When John arrived home, he covered himself with medicine and baked his clothes in the oven to kill any live insects. In spite of his sufferings, John knew he had done his best for the army.

Colonel Irvine. In one letter, Irvine wrote about his troops, "The Pennsylvanians think themselves inferior to none in **Zeal**, Bravery or Conduct."

On July 4, 1776, the Continental Congress met. The congressmen wanted everyone to know why they had **revolted** against Britain. The Congress wanted the citizens to know why the colonies should become free and independent states. At Congress' request, Thomas Jefferson of Virginia wrote the Declaration of Independence. This document stated that everyone was "created equal." It said the "Creator" had given each of them basic rights. And the Declaration said that, in order to guarantee these rights, the people should create and give power to their own government.

Even though Americans today take for granted that a government's citizens should create and control it, this idea amazed the colonists. Until the Declaration of Independence, Britain's king had ruled them. And

The Second Continental Congress asked Thomas Jefferson (standing) to write the Declaration of Independence.

now, in 1776, the colonies had to decide whether or not to support the Declaration of Independence.

Hundreds of women helped the Continental Army as America fought for freedom from Great Britain.

Camp Followers

The Declaration of Independence announced the birth of a new country. Ever since then, on each July 4, the United States has celebrated its birthday. But on July 4, 1776, the document acted as a declaration of revolution and war. It announced the colonies' break from a king who lived across the Atlantic Ocean, thousands of miles away.

General George Washington's young army fought hard against the British. But by December 1776, Washington could claim few victories. His soldiers seldom had enough to eat, and they often went barefoot. In a letter from 1776, Colonel Irvine complained about the lack of food, guns, and clothing. He said if his troops did not soon receive more supplies, he feared many of them would desert the army. One of his letters stated, ". . . Human Nature cannot bear being treated with **disrespect**."

On the evening of December 25th, General Washington planned a surprise attack on the British. He led his troops by boat from Pennsylvania across the icy Delaware River into New Jersey. That spot at the Delaware River where they crossed is still called "Washington Crossing." It lies not far from where Mary Ludwig Hays' childhood home stood in 1776.

The next morning, December 26, 1776, Washington's troops marched to Trenton through a violent snowstorm. In spite of the cruel weather, they attacked British forces and won. A few days later, Washington's soldiers won a second victory. But they still suffered from the severe conditions, including freezing weather, shabby clothing, and the lack of food.

By 1777, the army still suffered. Mary Hays heard

General George Washington led his troops across the Delaware River from Pennsylvania to New Jersey and defeated the British forces in Trenton.

about the pitiful conditions of the Continental Army. It upset her to know that her soldier-husband William was now suffering with the army. Many historians say Mary decided to ignore the people who said a woman should stay home and do only "women's work." Mary decided to join her husband and the other soldiers. She wanted to help them as they struggled for America's freedom.

Mary could do it, too. All the years of hard work

had made her strong in body, mind, and spirit. Also, she discovered she was not the only woman who desired to help the Continental Army. Hundreds of women had already begun to follow the troops. These "camp followers" would have a large role in determining whether America's army won or lost its struggle for independence. And Mary used her own strength to help decide the outcome.

In joining the fight for America's independence, Mary did not go only against society's expectations of women. She also went against the large number of colonists who did not want the Revolutionary War. But Mary was

I n addition to Molly, other women helped America win independence. An American Indian woman cooked and cleaned for General Washington during the Revolutionary War. One black woman rescued a colonist whom the British had captured. Another woman, Emily Geiger, on horseback, carried a secret message from one American general to another. Before she could reach the second general, enemies captured her. But before they could search her, she ate the message. When they did search Emily, they found no secret message, so they released her. When she finally reached the second American general, she recited from memory the message she had swallowed.

Camp followers accompanied Continental soldiers throughout the war. These women washed clothes, cooked, and tended to the sick.

not alone. According to records, from 1775 to 1783, about 20,000 women were camp followers during the war.

Many women who followed the troops were the soldiers' wives. Some of these women, while their husbands had been away at war, had lost their homes to British soldiers. Some of the women still had homes, but could not support their families while their husbands fought in the war. These camp followers followed and served the troops in order to survive and to help the American soldiers survive, too.

Except during combat, many of the camp followers worked harder than the soldiers. The camp followers performed the duties colonial society expected of women: washing clothes, cooking, sewing, and nursing the sick and injured. During many of the Revolutionary War winters, George Washington's wife Martha visited the camps and encouraged the women in their efforts to care for the soldiers.

Camp followers did not always get paid, but they always did earn their food from the army. Of course, they then had to cook the food, but many of them followed the troops for more than their daily bread. They followed the soldiers out of love and out of a need to be near them. They also followed the troops because they wanted to support the struggle for freedom.

General Washington always needed more soldiers to fight against the British. He usually could not afford to spare any of his men to act as cooks, laundry people, and nurses. The army

Martha Washington visited the army camps and encouraged women in their efforts to aid the soldiers.

relied heavily on the camp followers to provide these services.

In fact, some historians believe the Revolutionary War could not have been won without the support of camp followers like Mary. But not everyone appreciated these women. Sometimes, for example, their presence embarrassed George Washington. Before his troops marched through a large town, he often ordered the camp followers to take a different route. He did not want the presence of the loud, dusty, trail-worn women and children to make his troops look bad. He would order the women and children to march around the city instead of through it. On one occasion during the war, Washington issued this order, "Not a woman . . . is to be seen with the troops on their march [through] the city."

Imagine how Mary felt when she was not allowed to follow the soldiers through a town. She and the other camp followers worked hard to care for the men.

Even under the best conditions, Mary and the other women sometimes found their jobs as camp followers almost more than they could bear. Usually only pregnant women, officers' wives, and the sick and injured were allowed to ride in army wagons.

The majority of women had to walk along the rough trails, in all kinds of weather. Many of them, like many of the soldiers, went barefoot. Mary, too, went barefoot during part of the war.

In the summer and early fall of 1777, General Washington's army scored several more victories over the British. But his soldiers then lost some battles in Pennsylvania. By the time Christmas arrived, Washington and his troops huddled in misery at Valley Forge, Pennsylvania.

Mary Hays' former boss, Dr. Irvine, served as colonel in the 7th Pennsylvania Regiment in which Mary's husband served. Irvine and his men, including Mary's husband William Hays, were at Valley Forge during that terrible winter of 1777 through 1778. And Mary—as well as the other camp followers—cared for the suffering soldiers there.

At Valley Forge, during Pennsylvania's bitter winter, almost half of Washington's troops had no blankets. As many as one out of every three of them had no shoes. Washington's troops grew weaker every day.

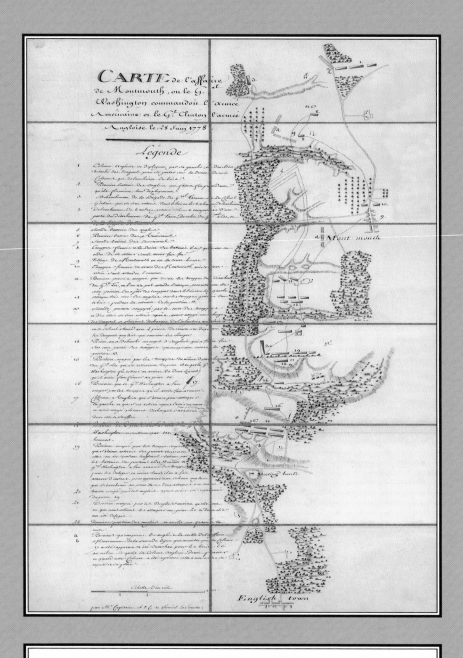

This map shows the Battle of Monmouth, New Jersey. Mary fought the Continental Army's thirst by carrying water onto the battlefield to the soldiers fighting the British in the summer heat.

Mary Ludwig Hays Becomes Molly Pitcher

The Continental Army fought no battles against the British during the winter at Valley Forge. But the army fought other battles. They battled hunger, freezing temperatures, and disease. The "Women of the Army," as General Washington called them, fought these battles alongside the men.

Throughout the Revolutionary War, the soldiers did not have enough food, clothing, and shoes. The army could not afford to meet their needs. During the bitter winter of 1777 through 1778, many soldiers suffered from illnesses and many died. But the ones who lived often thanked the women who served them. The camp followers had helped those soldiers survive.

Like Mary Hays, colonial society expected women to serve as wives and mothers—and nurses. These women held no medical degrees, and yet they had to treat the sick and wounded and try to save the dying. The Continental Congress appreciated the role women played in the army. Congress believed that without its "good female Nurses," the sufferings of the sick and wounded soldiers would grow worse.

During the winter at Valley Forge, General Washington issued many orders. In one of them, he told the army to get "as many Women of the Army as can be **prevailed on** to serve as Nurses." Like most women in colonial America, Mary could serve as a nurse. The women had learned much of their medical knowledge from their mothers and other women. In addition, Mary also might have learned how to help the sick and injured from her life at Dr. Irvine's house in Carlisle. During the winter at Valley Forge, camp followers probably used medicines based on natural ingredients like herbs.

From Valley Forge, General Washington wrote the Continental Congress about the soldiers' conditions at Valley Forge. He said they huddled on "a cold, **bleak** hill," and slept "under frost and snow without clothes or blankets. . . naked and **distressed**. . . ." On some mornings, soldiers even woke up with the hair on their heads frozen to the ground. If they suddenly lifted their heads, they would receive an instant, painful haircut. It is said that Washington told a friend, "Through the want of shoes and stockings, and the hard frozen ground you might have tracked the army. . . by the blood of their feet."

Even the shabby log huts some of the soldiers had built for themselves and their families did not completely protect them. Mary often had to sleep on the bare ground in these huts. Imagine Mary and William Hays huddling together on

Most camp followers led a hard life. In 1777, General Washington told his soldiers to get rid of any women not necessary to the army. He also wanted the soldiers to send home pregnant women and those with children. But when some women had to leave, their men left too. Washington could not afford to lose even one soldier. Most of the camp followers who were allowed to stay helped keep the soldiers and camps neat and clean. But a few followers threw garbage everywhere. Some even brought chickens with them, which caused a noisy mess wherever the animals went.

the frozen floor of a hut, trying to keep each other warm. The women, along with the soldiers, suffered from lack of clothing, weapons, equipment, and food that winter. Sometimes they had only flour and water to use in cooking. They mixed these together and baked them into tasteless flat cakes.

In spite of the brave and constant efforts of camp followers, many soldiers died that winter on that "cold, bleak hill." But many more survived, including Mary's husband. No army ever showed more bravery and dedication to their country than did the men and women at Valley Forge.

To the surprise of many, the cruel winter at

George Washington is pictured here overlooking the encampment at Valley Forge.

Valley Forge acted as a turning point for the Continental Army. For those who did not give up, did not quit, and did not die, their sufferings toughened and prepared them for their next challenge: the Battle of Monmouth. This famous battle would take place in New Jersey, not far from Mary's childhood farm.

While the Continental Army still suffered at Valley Forge in 1778, France decided to help America in its struggle for independence. This was great news for the Americans.

Later that year, British forces began to advance toward New York from Pennsylvania. General Washington ordered his army to follow them. They caught up with the British at Monmouth, New Jersey. Here on a sizzling-hot day in June 1778, Mary Ludwig Hays earned a place in American history as "Molly Pitcher."

Today, historians argue over what Mary "Molly Pitcher" Hays actually did during the Revolutionary War. A few even say Mary never was Molly Pitcher. Others argue that the name "Molly Pitcher" referred to hundreds of women during the War who carried pitchers of water to the fighting soldiers. In fact, several women besides Mary were called "Molly Pitcher." But most records claim Mary Ludwig Hays was *the* Molly Pitcher commonly referred to in history books.

How did she gain this greatness? During any Revolutionary War battle, a soldier operating a cannon needed a constant supply of water for two reasons. One, in order for his cannon to work properly, he had to clean the barrel with a wet sponge on the end of a sturdy pole. He did this after every shot he fired. The wet sponge removed sparks and material left from the cannon's last blast. Always short of manpower, the Continental Army relied on camp followers like Mary Hays to bring the needed water to the soldiers.

Every soldier needed water for another reason, too. During battles, especially the one at Monmouth on that hot day in June 1778, the soldiers were constantly dehydrated. They were constantly perspiring. If the soldiers did not get water, they could die. The Battle of

British forces advanced from New York and headed toward Pennsylvania. The Continental Army met the British at Monmouth, New Jersey, in June 1778.

Monmouth lasted from 11 in the morning until dark, which was a long time to fight a battle in such heat.

One doctor said some soldiers during the

Monmouth battle suffered so much from thirst, their tongues swelled up, and they could barely speak. At least 50 soldiers died that day just from the record-breaking heat.

Mary Ludwig Hays spent her life helping others. After the war, a friend said that Mary was not pretty or ladylike. But the friend also said Mary was always "ready to do a kind act for anyone." At the Battle of Monmouth, Mary risked her own life in order to help the fighting soldiers, the sick, and the dying.

On that famous day at Monmouth, for almost 12 hours, the British and American soldiers fired ammunition at each other. In the middle of the smoking guns and loud cries of soldiers as they fought, Mary continued to bring them water. The thirsty and exhausted soldiers, not knowing her real name, cried out, "Molly, bring me the pitcher." Or in their suffering, some soldiers may have only shouted, "Molly—the pitcher." In the intense heat of that June day, soldiers began to call for Mary's help simply by crying, "Molly! Pitcher!"

Years later, one woman who lived in Carlisle across the street from Molly said, "I heard her say she carried water to the men on the battlefield. . . . She was known pretty commonly as Mollie Pitcher; that was what we called her."

During the Monmouth battle, Mary "Molly Pitcher" Hays looked after her husband's needs, as well as those of other soldiers. That day, William Hays manned one of the Continental Army's cannons. Mary, covered with grime and dust, often stood beside him. During her service to the army, she must have learned from him and other soldiers how to load, clean, and fire a cannon. This knowledge served her well on that scorching day in June 1778.

William suddenly collapsed on the ground. The heat or exhaustion—or both—had probably overcome him. But Mary—now Molly Pitcher—

This engraving shows Mary at the Battle of Monmouth. She took over for her husband when he collapsed at his post. It was also during this battle that Mary earned the name Molly Pitcher because she carried pitchers of water to fighting soldiers.

took her husband's place at the cannon, risking her own life in order to join the battle for America's independence.

Women followed the army and took care of the sick and wounded soldiers.

Captain Molly Forever

F ighting at the Battle of Monmouth on June 28, 1778, would have made the soldiers hot even if the weather had been cool. But under the unusually high temperatures, many soldiers fell to the ground, overcome by the heat. The heat knocked down Molly Pitcher's husband, too.

With William sprawled on the ground next to her, Molly–again and again–cleaned, loaded, and fired his cannon at the British. Her early years of hard work on the farm, and then at Irvine's home, had strengthened her for this task. And the cruel winter at Valley Forge had strengthened her determination to do what she could to help America gain freedom.

Years later, a woman in Carlisle who knew Molly Pitcher remembered what Molly had said about the Revolutionary War: "You girls should have been with me at the Battle of Monmouth and learned how to load a cannon."

The day after the battle, General Washington sent a message to his troops. It said, "The Commander-in-Chief congratulates the Army on the Victory" over the British. Some records show that on that same Monday, General Greene presented Molly Pitcher to Washington. Some say Greene told him about her brave deeds, and Washington gave her the title of an officer. Even if that incident with Washington did not happen, many people, after the Battle of Monmouth, began to call Mary "Captain Molly" as well as "Molly Pitcher."

Two days after the battle, Washington ordered his troops and camp followers to pray. He told them to get together and give thanks to God for their victory at Monmouth.

Molly never forgot the fighting and suffering of the war. She was proud to have played a part in the fight for freedom.

One woman later stated that her soldier-husband often talked about the sufferings at the Battle of Monmouth. He told her, ". . . Captain Molly was busily engaged in carrying canteens of water to the **famished** soldiers. . . ."

Years after the war, Wesley Miles wrote in *The Carlisle Herald* about Molly and the Battle of Monmouth. He said she, "with a pitcher and water in hand . . . stood bravely near her husband." Wesley said when William fell on the ground, next to his cannon, Molly "took his now vacant place." Wesley told how she began to fire her husband's cannon at the British, "despite danger" and the "deafening roar of **artillery**."

After the Battle of Monmouth, poets praised Molly Pitcher's brave deeds.

> "All day the great guns barked and roared;
>
> All day the big balls screeched and soared;
>
> . . . Sweet Molly labored with courage high,
>
> With steady hand and watchful eye,
>
> Til the day was ours, and the sinking sun
>
> Looked down on the field of Monmouth won,
>
> And Molly standing beside her gun.
>
> Now, Molly, rest your weary arm!
>
> Safe, Molly, all is safe from harm."

Finally, in 1783, the colonists gained total victory over the British. The 13 colonies had finally won the struggle for independence. And Molly Pitcher had helped gain that victory.

At the end of the Revolutionary War in 1783, the Hays family returned to Carlisle to live. William and Mary had welcomed the birth of their only child, John L. Hays, in 1780. Some say that the "L" stands for "Ludwig," Molly's parents' last name. William again worked at his barber business. Molly worked hard to care for three year old John and his father.

In 1785, Pearce Rannals, an army veteran, came to live with William and Molly. According to records, Pearce pretended he was William's brother whenever Pearce visited local stores and restaurants. There he charged his expenses to William's accounts. Soon Pearce put William and Molly deep into debt. Pearce then sneaked out of town, but not before stealing William's musket, gunpowder holder, and a pair of his buckles.

A woman like Molly often had to treat her family's illnesses with homemade medicines. She used ingredients like dandelion roots, peppermint, onions, chalk, and teas. When a family member needed surgery, a doctor—if one could be found—traveled to the house. Often the surgery took place on the kitchen table. Family members had to help the doctor, who might give the patient something hard like a bullet to bite on during surgery. This biting was supposed to ease the pain. But often, the pain increased, and the patient simply fainted—or died.

William died the next year. And because of Pearce's stealing, William's death left Molly with huge debts. Court records show she had to sell one-half of their lot in order to pay off those debts.

According to Carlisle's 1793 tax records, "Molly Pitcher" Hays married another army veteran, John McCalla. Now her name grew even longer: Mary "Molly Pitcher" Hays McCalla. Apparently, neither John McCalla nor Molly could write. When they had to sign legal papers, they always signed "X" instead of their names. As a result, officials had to record the couple's last name the way it sounded: McCalla, McCauley, McCauly, or McKolly.

John McCalla worked for the town of Carlisle, hauling stones and clay for the prison there. Unfortunately, John McCalla and Molly did not have a happy marriage. A Carlisle court document of 1794 shows Jane Anderson, one of Molly's neighbors, accused him of attacking her. John admitted he had attacked Jane. No one knows what happened soon after that to John McCalla.

But at some point between 1807 and 1810, he simply disappeared.

Until her death in 1832, Molly continued to live in Carlisle where she attended the Lutheran church. One person who knew her said that Molly was "small and heavy with bristles in her nose. . . ." Another person agreed "she was so rough and coarse," but also said, "the roughness was on the outside. . . she would always visit the sick and was always willing to sit up at night with the sick." In one of her jobs after the war, Molly took care of Wesley Miles's mother. In *The Carlisle Herald,* he said Molly was "careful of the sick" and enjoyed taking care of them.

Ten years before Molly died, Pennsylvania voted to give her $40 every year. They did this to reward her for her brave deeds during the war.

In her old age, Molly was almost blind in one eye. Her hair had turned gray, and she usually wore a striped skirt, a ruffled cap, wool stockings, and heavy ankle-high shoes. According to one Carlisle citizen, Molly was "healthy, active and strong, fleshy

Molly was rewarded with $40 a year from Pennsylvania for service to her country during the American Revolution.

and short [and] passionately fond of children."

Until shortly before her death, Molly continued to work hard. In the Carlisle records of 1813, it says the city paid her for cleaning, washing, and painting the city's buildings. And until her death on January 22, 1832, she lived with her son John and his family.

Four days after Molly's death, Carlisle's *The American Volunteer* said that she had "lived during the days of the American Revolution, shared its hardships, and witnessed many a scene of Blood."

The newspaper said that she always helped "the sick and wounded." The article ended by stating that many people hoped God would take Molly to heaven and reward her for her good deeds.

After Molly's funeral, *The Carlisle Herald* said about her, "She was buried with military honors . . . The heroine of Monmouth, Molly Pitcher. . . ."

Today, the Molly Pitcher Highway leads travelers to Carlisle, Pennsylvania. In Carlisle in 1832, friends and family buried Mary "Molly Pitcher" Hays McCalla. Today, a monument and cannon in Carlisle remember the part she played in winning the Revolutionary War. In Freehold, New Jersey, at the Monmouth battlefield, a memorial declares her bravery.

The first camp followers had **inspired** Mary Ludwig Hays to work for victory over the horrors of the Revolutionary War. Now Captain Molly Pitcher inspires others to work—without violence—for freedom from all wrongs.

America's history will always be richer
Because of the name of Molly Pitcher.

GLOSSARY

ancestor–a family member who lived in the past.

artillery–large guns mounted on wheels.

bleak–gloomy.

brethren–people who share beliefs; people supporting the same cause.

colony–land owned by a distant nation.

disrespect–rudeness.

distressed–troubled; suffering.

famished–when one has a great hunger or thirst.

flourmill–a building in which one grinds grain to make flour.

immigrant–someone who settles in a foreign country.

independence–freedom from another government's or person's control.

inspire–to encourage someone to do good things.

menial–work done by a servant.

musket–a long gun.

Patriot–one who supports and defends one's country.

prevailed on–persuaded to.

ramrods–rods used for pushing in the charge in a firearm.

recruiter–one who tries to get others to join the military.

revolted–protested, rebelled.

zeal–enthusiasm.

CHRONOLOGY

1754	In approximately this year, Mary Ludwig is born in New Jersey.
1768	Leaves home, about this time, to live in Carlisle, Pennsylvania, and serve the Irvine family.
1769	Marries William Hays on July 24.
1775	Revolutionary War begins.
1777	William Hays joins the Continental Army; Mary becomes a camp follower.
1777–1778	Mary and William suffer together at Valley Forge.
1778	Fights at William's side at the Battle of Monmouth. Mary earns the name "Molly Pitcher."
1780	Only child, John, is born.
1783	Returns to Carlisle. William works as a barber, and Mary keeps her own house and works as a servant.
1786	William dies.
1793	Marries John McCalla. (in approximately this year)
1807–1810	John McCalla disappears (within this period)
1822	Awarded $40 per year for life by Pennsylvania.
1832	Dies in Carlisle on January 22.

REVOLUTIONARY WAR TIME LINE —

1765 The Stamp Act is passed by the British. Violent protests against it break out in the colonies.

1766 Britain ends the Stamp Act.

1767 Britain passes a law that taxes glass, painter's lead, paper, and tea in the colonies.

1770 Five colonists are killed by British soldiers in the Boston Massacre.

1773 People are angry about the taxes on tea. They throw boxes of tea from ships in Boston harbor into the water. It ruins the tea. The event is called the Boston Tea Party.

1774 The British pass laws to punish Boston for the Boston Tea Party. They close Boston harbor. Leaders in the colonies meet to plan a response to these actions.

1775 The battles of Lexington and Concord begin the American Revolution.

1776 The Declaration of Independence is signed. France and Spain give money to help the Americans fight Britain. Nathan Hale is captured by the British. He is charged with being a spy and is executed.

1777 Leaders choose a flag for America. The American troops win some important battles over the British. General Washington and his troops spend a very cold, hungry winter in Valley Forge.

1778 France sends ships to help the Americans win the war. The British are forced to leave Philadelphia.

1779 French ships head back to France. The French support the Americans in other ways.

1780 Americans discover that Benedict Arnold is a traitor. He escapes to the British. Major battles take place in North and South Carolina.

1781 The British surrender at Yorktown.

1783 A peace treaty is signed in France. British troops leave New York.

1787 The U.S. Constitution is written. Delaware becomes the first state in the Union.

1789 George Washington becomes the first president. John Adams is vice president.

FURTHER READING

Dagliesh, Alice. *The Fourth of July Story.* New York: Aladdin Paperbacks, 1995.

Jones, Veda Boyd. *Alexander Hamilton.* Philadelphia: Chelsea House, 2000.

Kalman, Bobbie. *Colonial Times From A to Z (Kalman, Bobbie, Alphabasics).* New York: Crabtree, 1997.

Keenan, Sheila. *Scholastic Encyclopedia of Women in the United States.* New York: Scholastic Inc., 1996.

Knight, James E. *The Winter at Valley Forge: Survival and Victory.* New Jersey: Troll Associates, 1999.

Murphy, Jim. *A Young Patriot: The American Revolution as Experienced By One Boy.* Massachusetts: Houghton Mifflin Co., 1998.

Quackenbush, Robert M. *Daughter of Liberty: A True Story of the American Revolution.* New York: Hyperion Press, 1999.

INDEX

PICTURE CREDITS

ABOUT THE AUTHOR

EILEEN DUNN BERTANZETTI has published more than 130 short stories and articles—as well as many books—for readers of all ages. She most enjoys researching and writing nonfiction. Since 1989, Eileen has taught adults how to write for children. With her husband Greg and their dogs Huckleberry Hound and Oggie Doggie, Eileen lives in Pennsylvania. Eileen and Greg enjoy their three grown children and six grandchildren.

Senior Consulting Editor **ARTHUR M. SCHLESINGER, JR.** is the leading American historian of our time. He won the Pulitzer Prize for his book *The Age of Jackson* (1945), and again for *A Thousand Days* (1965). This chronicle of the Kennedy Administration also won a National Book Award. He has written many other books, including a multi-volume series, *The Age of Roosevelt.* Professor Schlesinger is the Albert Schweitzer Professor of the Humanities at the City University of New York, and has been involved in several other Chelsea House projects, including the Colonial Leaders series of biographies on the most prominent figures of early American history.

ACKNOWLEDGMENT

My thanks to Jim McAvoy, Veda B. Jones, Greg, Andrea, Teri, Merri Lou, Annie Halenbake Ross Library, Cumberland County Historical Society, and Centre County Library.